COPING

By Kaytlin Dysart

ISBN-13: 978-1548422097

ISBN-10: 1548422096

Contact the Author
  Twitter: msinsomniac

Instagram: ms.insomniac

Snapchat: sgtcbaby

Chapter 1: Because I'm Different

Rikki slouched down in her chair.

"Well I don't know, sounds like she's on her own y'know." Rikki was the meanest one, no one really knew why, it's not like there was any trauma to make her that way, she was just mean. Kitty yanked the lollipop out of her month.

"I wanna help! Imma good helper! Right big bruder?" Kitty had all the childlike wonder, she was sweet and kind and so short that Imogen sometimes called her the terror on toothpicks. He wasn't her brother but she couldn't pronounce his name so he just answered to that. Imogen pulled her into his lap and patted her hair and smiled at her.

"Rikki if you're not going to be useful then leave, there's no need to sit here and be upset? I mean..." Imogen's voice was stern. Rikki angrily got up and and got in his face.

"You think you know so much don't you? Since you're the oldest?" She pushed his head to the side, walked into her room and slammed her door. Zane slumped in his seat yawned while looking at his phone.

"Why do we even have her at these meetings? She's only been helpful like 3 times, God she's such a hot head?" Zane was probably the one that cared the least, he wanted to be helpful but never knew how to be, so he normally thought it'd be best to keep quiet until he had something useful to say.

"I think she should just drop it. I mean he said sorry right? They should just kiss it out." Courtney was always the one who tried to keep the peace, she was a love conquers all type of person. Kitty jumped out of Imogen's lap and walked off to wander the halls.

"I think we should get rid of Rikki, I mean she's not useful at all, all she does is flip shit and leave." Zane said.

"I get it Zane and I'll talk to Katt about it. I mean I'm not sure it will blow over well thought." Imogen said.

"She's not that bad, I bet when the times comes she will be exactly what we need." Courtney said. Imogen got up to look for Kitty, finding her near Tak's door.

"Big bruder? Why doesn't Tak come out and play like everyone else?" Kitty asked as she looked at the pitch black door. Tak wasn't anti-social she just isn't received well by the others. She's comes out at special times and is actually the oldest, but since she's constantly forgotten that title falls on Imogen.

"She's not that friendly, little one." Imogen said as he picked her up and walked hastily from the dark hallway as if the darkness would pull him back if he didn't escape quickly enough. He opened Kitty's door and laid her down under her princess Tiana bed spread. He tucked her in and kissed her forehead.

"Promise me you won't bother Tak." Imogen said.

"I promise; can I play with her when she comes out?" Kitty asked, her big brown eyes pierced his soul.

"Sure goodnight" he walked out and closed the door quietly while turning out the light, as he turned around he came face to face with Katt.

"Hey" said Katt.

"Hey Katt" Imogen replied.

"Heard you guys arguing earlier, you shouldn't be so loud, you'll wake the neighbors," Katt laughed.

"What neighbors?" Imogen asked as he pushed past her and opened the door to his room. He sat down on his bed, Katt jumped in head first and stretched out.

"Don't you ever bother the others?" Imogen asked.

"Well I actually came to play with Kitty but..." Katt Looked away.

"Well try to show up during the day."

"You know I can't do that, it's uncomfortable." Katt sighed and got under his covers.

"I guess, so since you couldn't bother her you decided to bother me?"

"You're the only one that lets me in" she smiled. "Cut the crap, you can roam the house, you just choose not to." he rolled his eyes.

"It's mentally exhausting, there's too much going on." She snuggled wrapped her arms around his other pillow.

"Yeah yeah, well the problem didn't really get discussed. We actually ended up talking about why Rikki still lives here." he said nonchalantly.

"Don't worry about it, the problem was resolved." Her voice was cold.

"Would it be possible to kick Rikki out? I mean she's…" he turned to see that katt was no longer there.

"Dammit, she's worse than Batman." He got up and remade his bed.

The next morning, they all sat in the living room, Zane reading, Kitty playing with dolls, Courtney clutching her watch, and Rikki lighting matches and dropping them on the floor. Imogen walked in and started stomping out the matches on the floor.

"Rikki, if you could not kill us all that would be great." He said, making sure all the matches were out.

"It seems we had a visitor last night." Zane said not looking up from his book.

"She always shows up when we're all separated." Rikki said lighting and throwing another match.

"I wish she would come and visit the rest of us more often, it's like she's never here." Courtney said while polishing the face of the watch. It was a gift from *him* (Katt's Boyfriend) so she always kept it close.

"Why come big sister never wants to play with me?" Kitty asked as her eyes began to water, Imogen pulled her into his lap.

"She actually came to see you last night." Imogen said avoiding eye contact.

"Really?" Kitty sniffed.

"Yeah really." He wiped her tears and poked the tip of her nose "ding dong."

Her cheeks turned candy apple red and she smiled, she poked his nose yelled "ding dong" jumped off his lap and giggled while running away, He stood up to chase her but stopped.

"She stopped by to tell us that the problem had been handled." He said not turning to look at them.

"If she can handle the problems then what does she need us for?" Rikki said sounding annoyed.

"Did you discuss the other thing with her?" Zane said finally looking up from his book.

"She had no reply, you know she'll say no." Imogen said.

"That doesn't mean we shouldn't try right?" said Zane.

"This isn't the time to talk about this, but she's probably needed, that's why. I guess" Imogen said.

"For what?" Zane started to raise his voice.

"There are some problems that she's useful for." Imogen said in a stern voice.

"But--" Zane contested.

"Everyone stays." Imogen yelled and left the room.

"You guys talking about getting Tak kicked out?" Rikki asked while stepping on a match.

"Something like that, love." Courtney said looking cautiously at Zane, he went back to reading his book.

"You know Katt won't go for that, we all need each other even though it seems like one of us is useless, y'know?" Rikki said.

"I guess...yeah." Zane said rolling his eyes.

"She knows more than us, we're together for a reason, making Rikki right in this situation," Courtney said getting up from her and heading to her room. Rikki put out her last match and followed Courtney out of the room, letting Zane process what they had just said.

Chapter 2: Because I'm not right in the head

Kitty knocked on Rikki's door looking for something fun to do, Rikki opened the door wearing a crop top that said "Heavy" with short basketball shorts.

"Hi" Kitty said while waving.

"What's up shorty?" Rikki said as she walked over to her bed and picked up her guitar.

"You wanna play freeze tag, or toilet tag?" Kitty asked.

"What is toilet tag?" Rikki started to sound annoyed.

"When you get tagged you sit in the shape for a toilet and someone has to flush you to unfreeze you."

"I'll give that a hard pass."

"Rikki?"

"What?"

"Why are you so mean?"

"Because… well, I don't know I'm just made that way I guess."

"Can't you be nice like big bruder?"

"No, and for the record he is only nice to you, everyone is, cause your short."

"So when I get big everyone will start being mean?"

"Pretty much squirt."

"I'm never getting big."

"That's the plan, don't worry about your age, it's just a number."

Just then there was a knock at Rikki's door.

"Rikki can I get my book back?" Zane called.

"No." RIkki yelled back.

"What? Why not? Are you not done reading it?"

"Nope, I burned it." Rikki said nonchalantly.

"Why?" Zane asked annoyed.

"I like fire, needed material and didn't wanna burn something of my own, sooo sucks to suck right?" She said laughing.

Rikki opened the door, pushed Kitty into Zane's stomach, and then threw the book at his face.

"Just busting your balls." she slammed her door.

"Ugh" He sighed "Why do we keep her around?" he asked himself.

Rikki was also the prankster of the group, everyone hated it, but not as much as Zane. Even though he pretended it didn't bug him, he would actually beat himself up for being so gullible. Zane returned to his room with kitty right on his feet, he laid down in his bed while Kitty stood at his door way.

"Do I have to go away now?" Kitty looked down at her feet.

"Oh, yeah, no come in, sorry." He said.

Kitty walked in and sat in a bean bag chair picking up one of the children's books that Zane had left on the lower level for her. Unlike everyone else's bedroom Zane's was more like a library, every wall was a bookcase with his bed right in the center, he didn't need a dresser for his things because his clothes lived on the floor. Dirty ones in a pile in the corner and clean ones scattered about in various places, some even on the bed. Imogen knocked at the door.

"Zane, please take Kitty to her room and come to the living room."

Zane opened his door, threw Kitty over his shoulder and began walking swiftly to her room.

"Nap time, toothpicks." He put her in her bed left her with a book and closed her door.

"What happened?" Zane asked Imogen as he walked into the living room.

"There's noise." Imogen replied with a serious look on his face.

"What do you mean noise? There's always noise." Zane said unconcerned.

"No Zane... NOISE!" Rikki said, pointing at Tak's door.

"Maybe she heard us talking about kicking her out." Rikki was sweating, she had heard the stories, but always figured they were just bullshitting her. She was the badass and that was that, being the last roommate to move in she figured there was nothing behind the black door. But now she full heartedly knew that Tak was real and the danger was all too real. Imogen looked at his phone Katt wasn't answering, this is why he hated being the one in charge, when shit hit the fan he wanted to run but he couldn't he had to stay and hold his ground. He tried to make his face appear calm as if he was thinking. Courtney stayed in her room, she was too afraid to face Tak again. She had one experience with her that had almost made her lose her life. She knew better than anyone else to stay out of Tak's way when she did come out.

Around the time that Courtney first moved in the house it was still a pretty quiet place. Courtney was sitting in the living room alone, she figured everyone was just in their rooms so she didn't question why it was so quiet. Suddenly she saw a girl walk into the living room, it was a girl she hadn't met yet, no one had told her about another girl being there other than Kitty.

"Hi, I'm Courtney. I'm new here." Courtney said extending her hand out.

Tak just started at her.

"Okay then." Courtney put her hand down "So what's your name? Are you new too?"

"So you're the fresh meat hanging around here? I don't think I like you too much." Tak's Voice was raspy.

"Aww, I'm sure we'll come to love each other." Courtney started to back away a bit.

"Have you seen the others, I got some business with them." Tak looked around.

"No I figured they were all in their rooms, but I can go find them if you want." Courtney was nervous.

"No you'll do just fine." Tak grabbed Courtney by the neck and slammed her against the wall. Courtney gasped for air as tears ran down her face. She was confused and scared, what had she said wrong? Who was this girl and why was she never introduced? Imogen ran into the room pushing Tak off while

Courtney was passing out from lack of air, the last thing Courtney remembers seeing is Imogen confronting Tak.

Chapter 3: Because I'm not okay

"How are you so calm?" Zane asked Imogen in a panicking voice he had only seen the incident between Courtney and Tak. It was enough to make him sleep with the lights on for nights. He knew she couldn't get to him in his room, but he still spent those nights dreaming of "what ifs", what if she could get to him? What would she do to him? If she did escape would she go for him first? What if she saw him? Was he now on her hit list. He wanted to save Courtney, but Tak was scary and he lost his nerve. While his nights were filled with fear and his days' guilt because of how Courtney had changed. The ways she now clung to life instead of just living it freely like she used to.

Imogen turned to see tears streaming from Rikki's eyes.

"It's okay, noise doesn't always mean that she'll come out. I promise I won't let her hurt us," Imogen said.

"Why can't we just get rid of her?" Rikki asked.

"Because Katt says she stays dammit, and Katt is law." Imogen replied.

The noise behind the door settled back into a snore. The group eased closer to put their ears against the door.

"Next time" Tak said.

The 3 of them stepped back almost stepping on top of each other. Zane looked at Imogen while leaning against the wall for support, Imogen turned to Rikki and wiped her tears, she closed her eyes, exhaled, opened them then smacked his hand away.

"Don't be putting your hands on me, I ain't Kitty, I can take care of myself." She walked off quietly instead of her usual stomping. Even though she gave him trouble, Imogen knew that Rikki cared about all of them deep down inside. Imogen returned to his room, cranked up his AC and got under the covers. The cold reminded him of the days between fall and winter when the leaves were slowly switching to snowflakes, those days when no one really wants to be bothered so they don't really go out much.

Katt strolled into the living room, Rikki, lighting and tossing matches, Zane reading a romance and Imogen sat there. Imogen had dark circles under his bloodshot eyes he looked like he hadn't slept in several days.

"Hey" Katt said casually.

"Don't hey us!" Zane looked up from his book

"Yeah, you got some nerve showing up now after all the crap is over." Rikki said.

"Oh… right about Tak sorry about that guys." Katt acted like it wasn't a big deal.

"What the hell do you mean sorry? Why do you even keep her around? She's almost killed one of us before." Rikki was livid.

"Because she's useful that's why, stop worrying so much about each other and do your damn jobs." Katt wasn't normally such a hot head in front of them. She was five foot one not too fat not too skinny. She was just Katt and that's how she described herself.

"Our jobs don't involve almost getting killed?" Rikki stopped flicking her matches.

"Courtney was almost hurt really bad." Zane closed his book.

"You agree with them?" Katt looked at Imogen. He sighed, "I mean, we don't know how to deal with her, and you never answer when it's happening"

Katt puffed up a little like she was about to explode, Imogen quickly interjected. "But maybe we should have a protocol for those type of problems I mean…"

Katt sighed, "Fine. We'll get a routine in order or something alright? Any other matters to discuss?"

"Yeah, why the hell is she allowed to stay here? She's dangerous." Rikki stood collarbone to face with Katt.

"Because I said so that's why." Katt wasn't backing down.

"That's a bullshit answer, and you know it is." Rikki raised her voice.

"Are you questioning me?" Katt looked her up and down.

Imogen stood up and pulled Rikki away. "No, Katt we're fine, thanks for listening we'll see you later." He pushed Rikki back to her room leaving Katt and Zane.

Katt sat next to Zane and sighed, "I don't mean to be so bossy." She sounded sad.

"Well you have to be to do this job yeah?" He went back to reading his book.

"Yeah, you all probably hate me right?" She sighed and laid against his shoulder.

"That's humanly impossible?" He was barely paying attention.

"I guess you're right. Reading some romance?" She took the book out of his hand.

"I like to read it every once in a while, I feel all genres should be explored." He looked un-phased.

"How do I make things better?" She flipped through the book.

"You only seem to trust Imogen and Kitty, but we're all here and we all help?" He held his hand out for his book.

"Yeah, well I gotta get back, spending time here takes a lot out of my day." She gave him back his book, ruffled his hair and disappeared.

"He was right; she is just like Batman." Zane got up and walked back into his room.

Imogen was exhausted, he knew Katt was all knowing and such but he wondered why he listened to her so much. She was unimportant, no more than a landlady. But for some odd reason he just felt that he had to listen to her. It's not that she wasn't significant it's just that she wasn't normally like this, she was usually more easy going. He thought back to when he first meet Katt, he wasn't really quite sure what to think of her. She said she was a friend and would always be there when he needed her and that's how it was. Whenever they had issues they could run to each other, they grew up together and told each other secrets. They were the best of friends, Katt was always around and as they got older things got a little complicated, Katt stopped coming, boyfriends happened and school happened, Imogen eventually got really lonely.

"I'm gonna bring you some friends." Katt said excitedly.

"Friends? Why?" Imogen sounded uncomfortable.

"So you don't get lonely while I'm gone." Katt said.

"A lot of friends? How many? We don't have room." Imogen was worrying now.

"Don't worry about that, we'll make room, it'll be like a big sleepover all the time." Katt said.

"Won't more friends mean that you won't need to talk to me anymore?" He said.

"Of course not, we're best friends forever, inseparable almost like twins." She smiled.

They hugged it out and Imogen started wrapping his head around the idea of friends, he had never had any and only knew about Katt's friends. First came Kitty, she was a little shy at first because of his cold exterior but they eventually warmed up to each other. Zane followed, he didn't speak at all at first, but eventually started saving a sentence every few days. Courtney was quick to make friends and wanted to be with everyone all the time, she loved everyone and everything, the house, the roommates, and even though Rikki was mean to her, she loved her too. Rikki came in mad and stayed that way, she never really warmed up to anyone and still is the the new kid in a sense. No one knows when Tak appeared and no one bothered to ask either. Imogen was aware that there was something else there with him, though he wasn't quite sure what, but as long as it didn't bother him he wouldn't bother it. Imogen always knew why he was around and how helpful he was to Katt, but now it felt a bit crowded to him.

Katt walked into Kitty's room and closed the door behind her.

"Hi Kitty, I came to play with you." Katt said.

"Yeah cut the bullshit Katt, and you have to stop showing up around my bed time, the others might get suspicious" Kitty was serious.

"Of…?" Katt asked.

"Of who I really am, and that's a lot of work, so stop it." Kitty said sounding like she was about to throw a tantrum.

"Yeah, yeah, whatever, it'll be be fine." Katt pulled a book off Kitty's shelf and flipped through it, "Your idea of literature is a little dull for my preference."

"So what are we going to do about Tak?" Kitty sat in her bean bag chair and crossed her legs.

"Yeah, where did they put you, half pint?" Katt asked.

"Don't worry about that, just know that I was fully aware of the situation. She's becoming a problem and eventually that door won't keep her in." Kitty was not in the mood for Katt's jokes.

"Yeah, yeah, I know but how are we supposed to subdue her? She's the only one unwatched." Katt said.

Unlike the others Katt couldn't keep constant watch over Tak, Tak was something that Katt did not create voluntarily, so different rules applied to her. What those rules are, were unknown to Katt so when it came to Tak, she was always in unknown territory.

"Exactly why this is a problem, she could be planning her escape and we have nothing prepared." Kitty rested her hand on her cheek.

"Yeah, we'll get there, have the others figured it out yet?"

"No, not exactly, they're too busy fighting amongst each other, they are really different. I mean Rikki and Courtney are based off *your* boyfriend and you guys are complete opposites."

"Well they are ever changing, like us."

"You mean you?"

"Yea I guess..."

"Katt, eventually you'll have to tell them the truth. Maybe it will ease some of the tension."

"Soon." Katt got up and walked out of Kitty's room turning around to face Courtney.

"Oh hello love"

"Hi Courtney, how are you feeling?"

"Better." Courtney wasn't making eye contact, Katt was almost a little nervous that Courtney might have heard them.

"Well maybe you should get some more rest? You still seem a bit tired."

"Your right love, and thanks for tucking Kitty in, she's always talking about you."

"No problem, it takes a village or something like that right?" Courtney nodded and headed back to her room.

Chapter 4: Because I'm dangerous

Tak sat in her chair staring at her door. Her room was evergreen and had broken furniture surrounding her. The door was covered in scratch marks starting at the top reaching all the way to the bottom. Her knuckles blooded from punching the door. A single light bulb hung from the ceiling. Tak didn't need much light, didn't much care for it really, she always keeps a toothpick in her mouth, her hair was left in its natural state.

The next day Katt called a meeting, everyone came out of their rooms and sat quietly, it wasn't rare for Katt to call a meeting, but something about this meeting felt a little different, as if it was more of an announcement instead of the usual, which was Katt giving out problems for them to solve with a close deadline.

"Hey guys, I know there's been a lot of tension around here so I came to clear that all up." Katt stood in front of them.

"That's the understatement of the year." Rikki flicked her match at Katt's foot.

"Shut up." Zane punched her shoulder.

"For some odd reason you all have forgotten, but your multiple personalities of me." Katt looked around waiting for a gasp. "Figured I wouldn't surprise myself right? wow I'm an asshole to myself."

"Well we kind of already had an idea of it, but now we know why you can't really remove us though, so that's a problem solved." Imogen eased back comfortably in his chair.

"I have a question," Zane looked up from his book. "Why?"

"Because there are a lot of things in my life that I can't cope with so I compartmentalize, but instead of putting things in file cabinets I made people, also because I'm lonely as hell and need friends that understand me on the deepest level possible."

"You sound like a sad human being." Rikki giggled.

"So this means all of us are based off of someone or some problem in your life right?" Courtney smiled, excited to know her purpose in life.

"Yeah, technically, I mean if you really wanna know..." Katt said.

"That's what she asked," Rikki crossed her arms.

"I should work on that whole "being an asshole to myself" thing. Um okay, Imogen you're my alter ego, that's why we're like twins I guess. Rikki is the kick in the butt I sometimes need, and that normally comes from my boyfriend so they share a name, Courtney is all my love for Ricky, and Zane is the introvert in me and Kitty is my childlike wonder." Katt ran through it quickly.

"Well I do love Ricky a lot, he's like my special little shooting star, he never stops burning so bright." Courtney was really happy, her eyes, wide and her smile big across her face.

"I'm like your boyfriend? Gross!" Rikki said.

"Well it seems I over shot the whole encouragement part of him and just made you straight up mean. I meant to fix you but it seems to keep slipping my mind." Katt said.

"Don't fix what's not broken baby doll." Rikki smiled at Katt.

"Why tell us this now though?" Kitty asked.

"Well soon I'll be starting medicine"

"Medicine?" Imogen was concerned.

"Mental medicine. I'm depressed."

"So you're crazy?" Rikki was so rude about it.

"No, not crazy, not all humans are built the same, some of us don't have the same things as others, it's like genetics, not everyone is athletic or has brown eyes, it's just something that happens."

"But doesn't being depressed mean you're sad? I mean Ricky keeps you happy right? He's so nice to you." Courtney said.

"It's not about my life being bad at all, everyone's good to me, I just physically can't be happy my brain doesn't make enough of the happy hormone, and I shouldn't have to explain this to myself." Katt was getting frustrated.

"Obviously you do, to make yourself feel better." Zane flipped to the next page in his book. "You're not talking us into medicine you're talking yourself into it and making sure that this is what you want to do. You're accepting yourself as someone who needs help and that's cool."

Everyone turned to look at Zane, he looked up at them "What? We just found out we're all parts of her...I'm just saying what she's thinking because it's what we're all thinking." They all started laughing.

In the coming weeks Katt started her medicine and started seeing them more and more.

"Shouldn't you be at school right now?" Imogen asked as Katt walked into his room.

"Too tired." she got in his bed and tucked herself in.

"Yeah but you've missed like 3 days already, your mom's not gonna like this."

"Shut up." she closed her eyes and turned over, "And I missed two days last week and this is my second one this week, it's fine."

"You're missing a lot of important stuff."

"Look the truancy officer isn't knocking at my door, and I already made up last week's work."

"Participation is a grade too."

"Are you my conscience or my alter ego?"

"You tell me."

"Ugh." she turned over and pulled the cover over her head.

The pills had made Katt feel weird, she was always tired, so much so that she would sleep all day long, only waking up to eat, use the bathroom and shower. Even though she came to visit everyone all she did was sleep the whole time. She didn't have to go there to sleep but it made her feel better to be surrounded by her "friends" at this strange time in her life.

"All you do is sleep." Rikki said walking into a snoring Katt in her bed.

"I just feel really tired you know? Like I'm drowning in oxygen." Katt turned over.

"Well you need to get off your ass eventually." Rikki said pulling the pillow from under Katt.

"Yeah? Well maybe I don't wanna do that, sleeping is nice, no one can bother me this way." Katt yanked the pillow back.

"Sucks to suck! People are going to bother you until the cows come home, whether you're sleepy or not. Suck it up, moping around here won't make life any easier, if anything it would be worse for you if you mope around." Rikki yanked the covers off of Katt and pointed towards the door.

"Put an egg in your shoe and beat it. You're wasting away here, go be annoying elsewhere." Rikki pushed Katt out the door. Katt walked into Courtney's room to laid in her bed. Courtney's room was pink and fluffy, it was like walking into build-a-bear covered in pink and feathers. She had a waterbed, it felt like laying in a hot bath without getting wet.

"What's up beautiful?" Country said switching from her over head lights to two giant purple lava lamps.

"I just wanna sleep but Rikki's being my mother over there and I hate it." Katt said.

"Well, you have been extremely mopey, you keep lying about being tired but really you're just sad and lonely." she said.

"I ain't lonely." Katt yelled.

"Yeah, you are Hun. You walk around here bothering us to converse and hang with you, but you have so much to do out there, everyone's out there." Country pointed at the door.

"This is just fine for me." Katt whined. Just then Imogen walked in and threw her over his shoulder.

"You ain't gotta leave, but you gotta get the hell out of here." Imogen put her outside the door and shut it behind her. Katt patted her butt, got up and walked a dark hallway, she knew about these exits but she never really liked using it. As she headed to the strips of film of memories swam past her like eels, she hated being reminded of all these moments in her life at once, but this was the only physical way to leave this place.

"Kaytlin, Get Up! You ain't missing another day of school." her mom yelled.

Katt sprang into action started getting ready for her first day back in 2 days. Since Katt at felt better things started to go back to normal for a while

****

"I hate her!" Katt stormed into the living room.

"Trouble in the kingdom, Princess?" Rikki laughed.

"Shut up!" Katt yelled.

"Well what's the problem?" Imogen asked.

"My sister is the problem; everyone is constantly praising her." Katt laid down in the middle of the living room floor.

"Yeah... You should punch her." Rikki said.

"No, just sleep it off." Zane said still reading.

"No, never go to sleep angry, don't be upset when the sunsets." Country said.

"That's for couples and when you're going to bed, not naps, stupid." Rikki rolled her eyes.

"So naps don't count?" Zane asked.

"Everyone shut up, Katt just confront your family about the way you feel." Imogen said. Katt got up off the floor and walked into Zane's room.

"Yes, come in." Zane said sarcastically, he then got up and followed her, closing the door behind him.

"Whelp, not my problem anymore, I'm gonna go set something a blaze." Rikki started towards her room.

"Please refrain from killing us all." Imogen said and sighed.

Katt laid in Zane's bed and got up under his covers.

"Oh come on that's the best spot in the room." He laid down at the foot of the bed.

"And?" Katt said with her eyes closed.

"Ugh, confrontation…. Screw it I'm just gonna stay here, keep the spot." He said while reopening his book.

"What should I do?"

"I told you already, sleep it off."

"I can't do that."

"Do you really want advice or do you just want to no confrontational way to get out of this? Cause those are different things."

"I don't know."

"Ugh." he sighed and closed his book and went to get another one.

"Whatcha reading now?"

"Coming of age novel."

"Ahh, interesting."

"You're not leaving anytime soon are you?"

"I'll leave when I get my advice."

"No, you'll probably leave when you finally give up and accept that your older sister will always be better than you."

"Jeez, that's mean."

"Yeah, well it's true. You've been having this issue all your life and it will probably never stop. You have siblings. Deal with it."

"But I'm clearly better."

"Then what are you upset about?"

"They can't see it."

"Who?"

"Everyone, the whole family, just because she follows orders, it's crap!" Katt yelled.

"Are you gonna start following orders?"

"Hell no. why the fuck would I do that?"

"Okay, so then why does it matter?"

"Because they need to see my amazingness."

Zane sighed and turned on his stop to get more comfortable.

"You're literally the worst at this."

"Then go bother Imogen."

"He won't give me non-confrontational advice."

"Maybe because there is none, but if you want one then just let this go."

They laid there in silence, Zane was normally never this talkative but it made him extremely uncomfortable to have someone laying in his spot. He wanted her to go away but he knew he had to help her, he figured he would also be better at being helpful if he was in his correct sport. The little things meant a lot to Zane, he never said anything about though because there was never a need to, but still wished people would know.

Katt sighed.

"Now you're getting the hang of it." Zane chuckled. Katt got up and pulled a random book off the shelf, Zane quickly got up and jumped at his spot, when he landed he felt immediately at ease. Katt took his old spot and laid on her belly, they both laid there in silence.

"if you're not going to change, does it really matter what they think of you?"

"I guess not..."

"Then stop sweating it, let them love her, so then when she screws up it will come down harder on her, and when you do right they will praise you more."

"Sounds easy enough."

Zane didn't really feel like he gave her the advice she was looking for but he did tell her what she needed to hear. Why did she care if she wasn't going to do what he sister did? it was pointless. Katt didn't want to be like her sister she just wanted her family to praise her like they did her sister. Sooner or later Katt would outshine her sister so it would all work out eventually. Without confrontation.

Chapter 5: Because I am disjointed

The house began to shake like the aftershock of an earthquake it was small but still scary. Imogen knocked on Zane's door.

"Yeah?" Zane yawned.

"You feel that right?" Imogen asked.

"Yeah." Zane answered, he really wished he hadn't and tried to ignore it but he knew eventually he would have to deal with her. They all did. They walked to Courtney's door, before knocking Imogen and Zane exchanged looks before nodding. They had been talking about Courtney and them facing their fear. Country pulled the door open, eyes swollen and red from crying. After the incident, every time there was a hint that Tak might be on the loose Courtney would have anxiety attacks.

"I know." She said looking down. They all walked to Rikki's room and she was standing outside the door.

"Can we get this over with? I'm getting annoyed with having to hide like a child." Rikki spat.

"I agree." Imogen said ruffling her hair. Rikki slapped his hand away and rolled her eyes. They skipped Kitty's room hoping she was in her own imagination.

When the got to the door Kitty was already standing in front of it.

"Kitty, you shouldn't be here." Imogen said.

"Yeah yeah, I'm too young or whatever." Kitty said studying the door, ignoring the rest of what Imogen had to say. The house shook again but this time it was enough to make everyone lose their balance. Courtney ran to Tak's door and started kicking and punching it.

"Well come on with it then!" She yelled.

Rikki stepped back a few steps, she decided if she was going to get hurt she'd be the last one. Zane pulled Courtney away from the door and Imogen walked up to it, he exhaled slowly and looked back at them. Everyone looked just as worried. He turned the doorknob and pushed the door open. They saw Katt or a Katt-look-alike sitting in the chair hunched over.

"What is she" Zane said peering from behind Imogen's shoulder.

"A demon." Rikki said muffled.

"This isn't Tak" Courtney said said walking towards the unconscious Katt.

"But aren't they twins or whatever?" Rikki said.

"Well sort of, first off the hair style is different, so that's how we can tear them apart." Kitty exclaimed, they all turned to her.

"Secondly, see subconsciously we're all connected to Katt right? Well we are all voluntary made by her, everyone except Tak." Kitty poked Katt's body.

"So you're saying that what Katt originally told us was wrong?" Zane asked.

"Not exactly, she used us to deal with emotions when we're really just normal brain functions that everyone has, most of us are pretty much right, except for him." Kitty said pointing at Imogen. "also Katt did not voluntarily make Tak, She's just there."

"Imogen is the only one that is wrongly named." Kitty said.

"And what makes you so smart?" Rikki asked in a snippy voice.

"Because I am the subconscious, I see all and know all, even things that Katt herself doesn't know. Or at least pretends not to know." Kitty answered matter-of-factly.

"Then why do you look like a child?" Courtney asked.

"Because I am a child?" Kitty asked.

"Yeah, why?" Zane repeated the question.

"Because I am the part of Katt that doesn't change, no outside force can change me either, I do as I please or at least try to." Kitty smirked.

"So, If I'm not the alter ego then what am I?" Imogen asked.

"The conscience" Kitty replied. Kitty was aware that this illusion of them living as roommates was all fake from the beginning. But knew that that telling Katt the reality could have harmed her more then helped. Katt had known knew in the back of her mind that none of this was real.

"Why am I here?" Katt asked coming to "Oh God, where's Tak?" she asked.

"You tell us" Zane said.

"What the hell happened?" Courtney asked.

"Well I'm not exactly sure, something made me really mad and I'm not sure why but I couldn't control my anger, so here I am." Katt said unbelievably calm.

"Well you should probably get your body back" Courtney said.

"Yup, hold on." Katt closed her eyes and disappeared, suddenly Tak appeared in her place, and they all stepped back.

"Why are all of you in my room?" Tak said looking extremely angry.

"Because we're tired of you and your crap." Courtney stepped forward.

"Oh yeah? And what are you gonna do about it it? Lock me in a room and forget about me? You already tried that and now that I know how to get out you can't stop me." Tak grinned.

"We never locked you away." Imogen said.

"This is all your fault." Tak said walking up to Imogen.

"How?" He asked.

"You came along and I was no longer allowed to roam freely, I was unwanted as soon as she gave you a name." Tak went and sat in her seat.

"What are you talking about" Zane asked.

"Before you guys, there was me, Jim, Bob, and Selena, and we played with Katt all day long, then they disappeared and I was all alone. Then one day a room appeared when I walked into it the door shut and locked, I was trapped and have been there ever since.

But I could always hear all of you through the door, laughing and crying together I just couldn't join in." There were tears coming down Tak's face.

"Why did she lock me away?" She sobbed.

"Because you were dangerous and would hurt people" Kitty looked Tak in the eye. They had had a long history of dislike of one another. Tak was a dangerous person and during Katt's bouts of depression she was able to show herself more. Often making her have burst of anger over the smallest things. She would get angry with her sisters for small things like folding laundry even blowing up on her own parents. You made Katt come off as unapproachable and unresponsive."

"I see you're alive and well." Tak wiped her face.

"You were making her do and say mean things to people, so you were no longer allowed free reign. You were making her life harder with your disrespectful and uncaring attitude, making her push away people who were just trying to help." Kitty said.

"But who are Jim, Bob, and Selena, and why did you try to kill me?" Courtney wanted answers.

"Jim, Bob, and Selena were Katt's imaginary friends. But when she got a little older her mother said that she couldn't afford to feed them so they had to leave, so she sent them off to foster's home for imaginary friends." Imogen said.

"It's so sad that she had to have 3 Imaginary friends, I mean she has siblings, God she's a loser." Rikki laughed.

"I tried to kill you because you were the only one that could technically make matters worse for me. You are love, all of her love for *Him*. Love always trumps anger. Katt can't hurt me but *he* can. Also because I hate you all, you are all just stupid carbon copies of me! If I have to suffer so, do you. "Tak laughed maniacally.

"You deserve to rot you know that?!" Rikki yelled from behind Imogen

"How about I come interrupt your life instead?" Tak replied. Rikki flinched.

"Enough." Katt yelled.

"Oh look who decided to show up." Tak laughed.

"Sorry guys, I got a little held up dealing with mom, thanks for that by the way, not sure if I should eat dinner tonight." Katt looked at Tak. "Also I am not a loser my sister didn't play with me that's why I needed 3 imaginary friends so suck it Rikki."

"Whatever helps you sleep at night, Princess." Rikki Snickered.

"Shut up" Katt said. She turned back to Tak. "Listen I understand it's lonely in there, and that it's hard to suffer alone but you can't continue to be the way you are and want free roam, obviously locking you up won't do much either."

"So then what can we do?" Imogen asked.

"We could do that thing…" Kitty Looked at Katt with cautious eyes.

"I don't know if that would work so well since she's still part of me." Katt looked down feeling nervous.

"Well we have to do something, she can't keep wreaking havoc." Kitty said gesturing at Tak.

"There's nothing you can do with me. I will always escape, might was well let me reclaim my throne as the queen." She smiled.

"That's my job." Rikki retaliated.

"Well it looks like you've been fired." Tak spat back.

"Enough already. You both suck, also if I'm going to be ruled over I would prefer it to be Courtney, no offense to Katt." Zane said.

"I'm the queen because I am God here!" Katt yelled.

"Says you." Kitty said under her breathe.

"What was that dangerous thing you two were talking about earlier?" Imogen asked.

"Erasing her." Katt said with a blank face.
The whole room fell silent, everyone had looked at each other and then Katt. Because they had never seen anyone get erased they figured they couldn't die. They didn't much have a concept of death; they all knew Katt's feelings on it but never thought that they could experience it.

"Ha! If you could've erased me you would have done it before, you're bluffing." Tak laughed in Katt's face.

"That's not necessarily true." Kitty said.

"It's not that I couldn't, it's just that I never thought of it. I always figured that you were unchanging like Kitty, so even if I did you would just come back. But I never stop to think if you really are just what I really am or what I think I am. You're not me. I'm me." Katt said.

"So by that logic, she's no stronger than the rest of us." Zane stated.

All the color left Tak's face. It had felt like all her strength had been sucked out of her, she fell to the ground and looked up at the group, this whole time she thought she was internal, invincible. To know that she was nothing more than the ones she called carbon copies broke her. Katt looked at Tak with fierce eyes then closed them. It looked like she was focusing really hard, the lights began to flicker and the house shook a little. Tak let out a blood curdling scream, her hair became dust and her eyeball melted out of her sockets. Her skin cracked like porcelain as her limbs began to fall off, the screams continued until her body became a pile of bones and pieces of skin. Suddenly a hole to nowhere opened around her remains and sucked her in. Her door opened and all the contents inside were sucked backwards, the door then closed cracked down the middle and became dust, falling to the ground.

Katt opened her eyes to stares from the whole group. She hadn't seen what happened to Tak, just knew that she has wished that Tak would go away with all of her being.

"Well that was something I can't un-see." Rikki said looking horrified.

"Yeah I don't think I'll be sleeping for a while." Zane said looking down at his book.

For the first time Zane's face showed a different expression that didn't look bored. He was completely amazed and disturbed at what he just saw. Disturbed because it was mental picture that would always be with him and amazed that Katt had the amount of power. Courtney felt relieved that the person causing all her suffering was finally gone, she didn't even feel bad for how she went and felt that Tak deserved everything that she had coming. Rikki, thought she was the badass around but she now knows that she was and will never be the queen, but that didn't mean that she had to stop acting like it. Imogen felt a little sad for Tak, being the peaceful one he wanted her to repent and find a way to stay with the rest of them but at the same time he was happy to know that she could no longer torture him. Kitty was happy, all along she had wanted Katt to know that she didn't actually need them, that Tak wasn't actually as scary as Katt thought she was and Katt was the only one giving Tak power.

Chapter 6: Because I am Free

A couple of days after Tak's demise Imogen started to notice that Katt wasn't needing them for many situations anymore. At first he started to get scared thinking about the fact of her never coming back to see them again. What if she decided that she didn't need them anymore? That they needed to disappear just like Tak did? He called everyone in the house to talk about the problem.

"So I'm worried" Imogen started.

"About?" Kitty asked.

"Katt hasn't been here in a while." He said.

"Well, maybe she's busy? It's a new year and college applications are coming up soon" Kitty said.

"But normally when she's busy she's stressed right?" Zane asked.

"Exactly! So where is she?" Imogen replied.

"Maybe she's busy with *Him*" Rikki said.

"Yeah, they haven't fought in a while so maybe things are kind nice for her." Courtney agreed.

"But what if they stay nice? What if she stops needing us? And we disappear like Tak did?" Imogen's voice was shaking.

"She will always need us." Kitty said.

"How do you know? It's not like you've always had a body." Imogen accused.

"Stop before you cause panic." Kitty said calmly.

"He's right you know; it's not like we've always been here. What will happen to me and Rikki if things go sour with *him*?" Courtney asked.

"Wait, I could disappear?" Rikki asked cautiously.

"Well duh, Katt pretty much just showed us that everyone can disappear except Kitty." Zane said.

Just then Katt walked into the room quietly, they were bickering too much for anyone to notice her. Katt thought it was funny that figments of her imagination were worried about being sent away somewhere else as if they could be forgotten. Everyone that Katt had created throughout the years was special to her in their own way, even Tak. Though some weren't around anymore it didn't mean that they were forgotten it just meant that she had gotten past that part in her life. But Katt couldn't see her life without these guys, and didn't see *him* going anywhere any time soon. She walked up to the table and slammed her hands on the desk.

"Guys!" She yelled. They all stopped and looked at her.

"You guys are going anywhere! Just because I'm not constantly here anymore doesn't mean you're not needed, all my life's rough patches aren't over I'm sure of it. I'm not even 18 yet, and look at all the issues I've needed you all for. Every single one of you is important and is needed. Imogen where in the world would I be without my conscience? Jail. That's where. Zane, there's nothing wrong with being an introvert sometimes. Rikki, though you're not helpful, everyone has the right to be angry sometimes. Courtney, love is important no matter who it's for, your name may change but you won't. And Kitty let's be honest you can't really go anywhere because you've always been here. I guarantee that none of you will be forgotten." Katt said. The room busted with laughter.

"You're soo gushy!" Rikki Laughed.

"I can't believe I was so worried." Imogen chucked.

"I'm not sure what's so funny but I feel relieved." Zane said.

"Well I like my name, so don't go changing it too soon." Courtney laughed.

"But what about your imaginary friends? They're gone." Imogen asked.

"No, actually they're not. I couldn't bring myself to get rid of them. Also when I was a child my sister showed that movie *"Don't Look Under the Bed"* which is about how imaginary friends turn into boogiemen if they are forgotten so trust me everyone is safe. Jim, Bob, and Salena are a part of you guys." Katt smiled, looking away thinking about her fear of all of them being possible boogiemen.

"You're a child you know that?" Kitty said.

"More like a wimp." Rikki laughed.

"You know, there's nothing stopping you from following Tak." Katt threatened. Since everyone seemed have calmed down, Katt figured this would be a perfect time to leave, she decided to walk down memory lane this time instead. Imogen noticed she was leaving and decided to follow her out. They walked towards the exit quietly together just enjoying each other's company. Suddenly Imogen was guiding her away from the exit.

"Where are we going?" Katt asked.

"I found something the other day, and I needed to ask you this, I just didn't want to do it in front of everyone else." He said leading her down a hallway that looked unfamiliar.

"Um, this is new?" she said.

"Are you saying that you're not completely aware of everything going on in your brain?" Imogen asked.

"Well not *everything* like I don't pay much attention to the part that controls my motor skills, and sometimes my subconscious can do things that I'm not particularly aware of." Katt said sounded a bit confused. They stopped at a grey door that had blue stars around the border.

"Who's door is that?" Imogen asked.

"I'm not completely sure," Katt answered. "But, I'm sure we'll meet whoever they are pretty soon." She turned and start back towards the exit. Imogen knocked on the door curious to who or what was living behind it. A piece of paper came from under the door that read: *I'll come out when I'm ready, but until then shooo.*

Imogen tucked the letter in his pocket and smiled.

Chapter 7: Because I Am cured?

After walking back to the living room with everyone else Imogen pulled Kitty aside.

"So, since you're the subconscious shouldn't you be in charge?" Imogen asked.

"No, you're doing a fine job." Kitty replied.

"But it's your birthright technically." He said.

"If I wanted to be in charge I would have made myself known when you first appeared." She said sounding annoyed.

"But-" He stuttered.

"Imogen, if you were doing something wrong I would have revealed myself to you and fixed it. I am more of a behind the scenes person you know? I'm the stage hand that makes sure the show goes on." She smiled.

Imogen picked her up and hugged her, it made him feel at ease to know that even if he did mess up there was something there to make sure that everything would still be okay, almost like a mentor even though she still felt like his little sister. Soon the house when back to normal and everyone had regained their rolls, even Kitty started slipping back into being a child, though she no longer had bedtimes she still only showed her serious side when it was extremely important. Katt was back to her normal self too, at least as normal as she could get, she knocked on Courtney's door.

"Yes." Courtney opened her door, blowing her nails. "Oh it's you Katt." Katt's eyes were glazed over, it looked like she had been crying for hours.

"Oh honey what happened?"

"We haven't talked in like two days, where is he? Did he die? Does he not care about me anymore?"

"Hold on there, before you jump to a conclusion." Courtney sat in her fluffy bean bag chair. "Who? What? When? Where? and for how many cookies?"

"Ricky. We haven't talked in two days." Katt sobbed.

"Two days in your hours or two days as in 48 hours?"

"What's the difference?"

"Well one is 48 hours and the other is like 2 hours, your time is not real time Katt."

"Why isn't it?"

"Because it's 4 am, and you're an insomniac, your days all run together honey."

"Ugh, but where is he!? Why isn't he answering my texts?"

"Because its 4 am. He's probably sleep. Everyone can't stay awake like you honey... Remember?"

"That's stupid."

"And you're being a brat."

Katt sat on the bed and put a pillow on her face.

"What if he's with someone else?"

"Okay that's ridiculous."

"How do you know he's not?"

"Well, just an idea, stay with me, but its 4 am."

"I guess."

"Well I know. So it works out."

Katt sighed and wiped her eyes, she knew deep down that was being ridiculous, but she had never cared for someone so much. She wanted to talk to him all the time but alas he was a normal human who needed 8 hours sleep to function.

"I know he's not doing anything wrong. I'm just so sad."

"Well it's okay to be an emotional bunny rabbit from time to time?"

"An emotional bunny rabbit?"

"Hey it's your brain, that's what you refer to yourself as don't start questioning me."

"I am emotional that's for sure. Ugh… damn his need for sleep."

"Love is hard and annoying but it's all worth it! Soo why don't you go to sleep now, so when you wake up he'll be awake."

"Oh mah gawd, your right!"

"You're a child, you got snot and tears all over my pillow."

"Yeah, yeah."

Courtney sighed and smiled, she knows Katt genuinely loved Ricky, she just went a little overboard every once and a while.

Chapter 8: Because everything is never as it seems

While Courtney was dealing with Katt and her hilarious Ricky crisis the others had

begun to find things around the place a bit boring, until one day while sitting in the living room an unknown person walked in.

"Um… who the hell are you?" Rikki asked.

"I'm not quite sure." The stranger responded.

"You're not sure?" Imogen repeated.

"No, not really… Um I've been in what I assume is my room for a while now, and finally the door unlocked allowing me to escape." The stranger looked around the room.

"So you're the new one?" Kitty said walking into the room.

"New one?" Zane looked up from the book.

"Why?! Are we not good enough? Get your ass in here Katt! are we not enough!?" Rikki screamed shaking her fist at the ceiling.

"Calm down, I knew he was here, saw his door once while I was talking Katt out, I don't even think she was aware that she was making him." Imogen studied the stranger.

"Is he the new Tak?" Country sounded scared, "Can we be reincarnated?" She asked while stepping behind Imogen.

"Who?" The stranger asked.

"Okay, so do you know what you're supposed to do here?" Imogen asked.

"To help with the Depression right?" Stranger asked.

"Oh?" Kitty sounded surprised.

"This could be the Prozac." Zane chimed in.

"What do you mean?" Courtney asked.

"Well Imogen said that Katt was unaware of his being made right? remember she said she was going to meds to combat her depression? This could be what it does." Kitty explain.

"That can't be normal." Rikki said, the whole idea of having to share this space with another person made her feel annoyed and less useful.

"We're figments of imagination in a teenage girl's head, this was never normal from the start." Zane said. He liked the new guy, the stranger seemed a lot like him, not too lively. Courtney was always happy to meet a new person and felt like him being here could be great for Katt, since the depression made it harder for them to be helpful at times. That was because her depression is caused by an imbalance of chemicals in her brain and not trauma. Kitty was unsure how to feel about him, but she understood that he was needed, she was more curious about what his role was, was he a stage hand like her or a bigger player like the rest. Imogen had no opinion about the stranger at the time. The stranger on the other hand had a plethora of of mixed feelings about the others, how long have they been here? what do they each do? is exactly is Katt? they all seemed to have names, who was naming them and who was the leader when this Katt person wasn't around? What he did know though is that he preferred the guys over the girls, the girls were a little too lively to him, but that didn't make them bad people.

"So what do we name him?" Courtney asked.

"Well we're not his creator so we can't just name him" Imogen said.

"Let's call him Prozac." Rikki interjected.

"What did I just say Rikki? One job, just one." Imogen face palmed.

"Well we gotta call him something." Rikki responded.

"She not wrong." Zane said.

Imogen sighed. "Do you like the name Prozac?" He asked the Stranger.

"Well, what are your names? What do you do?" the stranger asked, sounding like he had ignored the question. Everyone went around the room stating their names and they bring to Katt's brain. The stranger thought it was stranger that they all seemed to not cover the depression aspect of Katt.

"So, question?" He asked.

"Answer." Rikki replied quickly.

"Why was I made? How come none of you can cover this part?" He asked.

"Because we were here before the depression, so we're not made to deal with it, so instead of adjusting up Katt must have made you." Kitty answered.

"Huh...interesting, and yes, I am fine with being called Prozac." Prozac said.

"Well that's what we'll call you until Katt renames you. if she does rename you." Kitty said.

"I'm fine with that, where is Katt?" Prozac asked.

"On the outside, we only exist in here, she'll come when she feels like it or gets the change too, whichever comes first. I sure she's aware of you now since we're aware of you now." Imogen said.

"Okay, well I guess I'll just wait in my room then." Prozac walked off into the hallway towards his room. The group looked at each other waiting for someone to speak.

"I like him." Zane said.

"He's a cool guy." Imogen said.

"Well let's hope he stays that way, don't get too close to him until Katt gets here, he might be short lived." kitty said and walked back to her room.

"He's way too quiet. Another Zane is the last thing we need." Rikki said crossing her arms.

"Actually the last thing we need is another hot head." Zane said.

"Enough you two," Imogen said.

"He started it…" Rikki went to her room.

"So what if he's dangerous?" Courtney asked.

"Then we we'll get rid of him like we did Tak." Imogen said.

"Before or after he tries to kill one of us?" Courtney asked and walked out to her room. Imogen didn't know what to say, Courtney seemed really happy about meeting Prozac, at first, now she was just scared.

"Just leave her alone for a while, she's a little sensitive since the last new comer meant bad news for her." Zane said closing his book.

"I know, and I want to make sure that it doesn't happen come that close again." Imogen said sunning his hand through his his hair.

"Some people need to face somethings on their own, it's not like she had too much closure over Tak's death, I mean how would you feel if someone said they just "felt" like killing you?" Zane really wanted to read his book but this was obviously something Imogen needed to get out.

"I mean I guess you're right, I just don't know want her to hate him before she knows him, it's not fair to him." Imogen said.

"And it's not fair to Courtney that someone tried to kill her, and we let that person hang around the after the fact." Zane snapped back, he's not normally one to get mad, confrontation was not his style but he had felt bad about what happened to her and felt even worse that he couldn't stop it.

"You're right, I'm sorry." Imogen looked down.

"I'm not the one you should be apologizing too." Zane opened his book and began to read again. Courtney sat in her fluffy pink bean bag chair. she was happy about Prozac at first but then she remembered what Tak did, what would happen if Prozac turned out to be dangerous. Prozac was not like them, he was in Katt's bloodstream, doing something to her brain. He had a real world connect that none of the rest of them had. if he had killed any of them how would he be stopped? It sounds like Katt can't like maybe she she is no longer the stronger one and that's what scared her the most. A knock at her door took Courtney out of her concentration.

"Come in." She yelled. Imogen opened the door and poked his head through.

"Is this a bad time?"

"No."

"I'm sorry if it seemed like I didn't care about your worries."

"It's really okay, I was just worried, it seems like no one is worried about him being dangerous."

"Well we're trying not to judge him, that's all. He might be a decent person you know?"

"Yeah, you're right."

"But I do understand how you feel and I will try to keep a close eye on him, no one will hurt you again." Courtney smiled and hugged him, she was happy that someone was listening and didn't just brush her off.

"Could you maybe talk to Katt about it?"

"I could try; I can't imagine her being mad or anything like that."

"Thanks."

Imogen got up and left her room, he was happy that he could be of use, for once in his life being the leader didn't feel like such a burden. He finally felt like he was getting the hand of the leadership crap. He walked happily back to his room and thought about how amazing his was. Zane walked into the living room and saw Prozac sitting there with his headphones on, his eyes closed, completely lost in the music. Zane sat in his chair and started reading, they sat in silence for a while until Prozac finally noticed Zane.

"Oh, sorry, I didn't notice you came in."

"It's okay, it's not like I really came out here to talk."

"Why did you come out here?"

"Because it's unhealthy to stay locked in my room err whatever, also I couldn't find a comfortable reading spot in my bed."

"Do you always read?"

"Yeah, it's the best way to keep my comfortable."

"What do you mean?"

"Reality is uncomfortable and confrontational so I live in my books so don't have to deal with it."

"Isn't that bad? Confrontation is sometimes a good thing."

"Oh, no, I do confront people, but if I don't have to I won't. I keep her anxiety in tact so she doesn't fall apart at the seams, there's no need to cause problems over little things, that could later become catastrophic."

"I guess that's true."

"One decision could almost always screw you over."

"Makes sense."

"So what's up with the headphones?"

"This place is way too quiet; it drives me insane."

"Really?"

"Music is comforting. Silence makes me paranoid, I'm not sure why but an Idle mind is the Devil's plaything."

"Hands."

"What?"

"Idle hands are the Devil's plaything."

"Same thing."

"True."

Prozac put his headphones back on and closed his eyes again. Zane had enjoyed his time with Prozac, he was calming, not loud and not bothersome. He had started to wonder why Katt had never made anyone like him before, maybe he would ask, or not, that seemed like too much work. Just then Katt had appeared in the living room.

"Hi Katt." Prozac said.

"How do you know who I am?"

"Well judging by the fact that I have already met everyone that lives here and everyone here has to walk everywhere and you just appeared here, it would be safe to assume you are Katt."

"Well you're not wrong."

"You're an interesting person."

"I am, so you're the new guy, I thought you would be a girl, I don't know why, but it makes sense that you're a guy, balance is important."

"If you say so."

"What are you listening to?"

"Ice Cube's 'today was a good day.'"

"That really fits my day, I didn't have to use my AK... I guess it was a good day."

"I repeat, you're a very interesting person."

"And so are you. So your name is Prozac?"

"That's what they call me."

"Do you want a new name?"

"What do ya got?"

"Just Zac, short for Prozac."

"Okay, I like that, from now on everyone can call me Zac."

"Ha, Zac and Zane, ha." Katt laughed.

"So can I help you or anything like that? Is everything okay?"

"Didn't you hear the music? Yes, everything is great."

"Oh, well, why are you here?"

"To meet you, of course, you have to know who you're helping right? Welcome to the brain gang."

"Lame." Zane said.

"Shut up." Katt laughed.

Katt was happy about Zac, she knew he was going to be good for her, and hopefully he would take away those unwanted thoughts she had.

"Well that's all I needed, bye."

"Seriously, that was it." Zac asked.

"Well yeah? I mean, I don't have any issues right now, sooo great meeting, brain orientations officially over."

"What, no batman-esk exit for him?" Zane asked.

"What?" Zane looked at Zane, Zane nodded to the now empty spot where Katt was standing. Zac looked over and saw she was gone.

"Normally she doesn't say goodbye."

"Cool! can we do that?"

"if only," Zane laughed. just then Imogen and kitty walked into the room.

"I have a taste for ice cream!" Kitty giggled.

"But we don't eat." Imogen laughed.

"Awwies."

"So did you meet Katt?"

"Yeah, so my official name is Zac now."

"Coolio, that's good."

"So when will she be back?"

"It's random, she could be back in 2 days or 5 minutes, but it's Monday in the real world and Katt hates Mondays so I'm sure she'll be back soon."

"Like Garfield." Kitty said.

"Why do you keep this up?" Zane asked Kitty.

"Because it's fun and I don't have to deal with grown up stuff unless it's important now shut your food hole and stop judging me." Kitty spat back.

"0 to 100" Zane said and went back to reading.

"Everyone calm down." Imogen picked kitty up and carried her to her room. "I know you're important but don't be rude, especially to Zane, if you do then he'll never leave his room." Imogen said patting her back.

"He's right." Zane chimed in while walking back to his room.

"And then there was one." Zac said, he got up and walked to his room. The blue stars were now gone, the top have of the door was pale green and the bottle half was white. He walked in, put his headphones on top of one of his many speakers that filled the room, grabbed the remote to his sound system and simultaneously clicked the on but while getting in bed. My Chemical Romances "I'm not okay" started playing, when the lyric "I'm not o-fucking Kay" enter his ear there was a knock at his door. He opened it to see Katt standing on the other side of it.

"What's wrong?"

"It's hard to do this."

"Do what?"

"Act like everything's okay."

"Is it not okay?"

"Nothing is ever okay."

"Um okay."

"Why can't I be normal"

"Because being normal is no fun."

"No, why do I have to be sad all the time."

"Because you have a chemical imbalance in your brain that stops you?"

"I should kill myself."

"You could but what would you gain?"

"Not having to feel."

"And you would lose your family and everyone important to you."

"I guess."

"Is it really worth all that?"

"I don't know."

"Better question, do you you feel like going through all that work?"

"No, I'm just sad."

"Do you know why you're sad?"

"No."

"It's okay to not be okay sometimes. you don't have to constantly be happy nor do you always have to have a reason to be sad. Emotions are not always fully rational."

"You're right." Katt laid in his bed.

"Um…"

"I'm gonna take a nap here."

"Right there?"

"Yeah."

"Okay take a nap"

"Okay, I will, night night."

"Good night."

The music in the room changed to sounds of Pharrell, it was calming and he liked it. This proved a theory that Zac had been thinking about since he had met Katt: her feelings from outside had direct effect on his music. This was good because now he could understand what Katt was experiencing on the outside first hand. But what did this all mean? He decided to go talk to Imogen and Kitty.

Imogen heard a knock at his door.

"Hello? It's me?" Zac Poked his head in.

"Hello from the other side." Imogen laughed and and gestured for Zac to come in.

"Hilarious, but anyways do you have time to talk?"

"If Katt's not in here then then I have all the time in the world."

"Well, Katt's music emotions are connected to my music, as in everything I listen to cannot be physically controlled by me."

"Well, that's interesting Katt's feelings normally don't affect us that much, they really only effect Zane's reading choices."

"How?"

"Just enough for him to decide which genres he picks up, nothing deeper than that, but he reads them for days so we can't be sure if those emotions are happening consciously or subconsciously."

"So the is the closest she's came?"

"Well, yes this could be due to the fact that you're based off of a pill that's supposed to help her control her emotions, have you heard any loves longs yet?"

"Well no, only happy and sad songs."

"So your music could possibly be connecting to her mental state, which is different than her emotions."

"Yeah, that could be true."

"Just keep listening for a couple days and then we'll really know what it is. Where is Katt? Do you know?"

"Taking a nap in my bed."

"Yeah, she does that a lot."

"Well then, I guess that's something I will have to get used to."

"Sometimes Katt feels it is easier to sleep away her problems and that involves her sleep here. She won't always be in your bed but assume so then you won't be disappointed when she is there."

"Got it, should I tell Kitty about this?"

"Nah, I will."

Zac closed the door behind him put his headphones back on and sat in his chair in the living room. Rikki came out with her guitar and started strumming it while sitting her chair.

"You like music?" Zac asked.

"Just making it."

"Do we all have something in common with each other?"

"I don't know. Probably, seems like something Katt would do, she's annoying like that."

"Do you actually like Katt?"

"It's a love hate relationship, she loves me, I hate her, so it works out."

"You think so?"

"If it doesn't am I supposed to care?"

"You're a strange person."

"No one care cares what you think."

While Rikki and Zac were getting more acquainted Imogen went to see Kitty about what's been happening the last few days.

"What's up?"

"Courtney was worried that Zac could be too dangerous to keep around."

"That's understand ale. she could be right, Zac is not like us, he has ties to reality."

"Well, what should we do?"

"Nothing, at least nothing right now, we can't just distrust him, we'll just have to burn that bridge when we get to it."

"Cross."

"Same thing."

"All apparently Katt's mental state has a direct link to Zac's music."

"That's interesting."

"Yeah, so he has the potential to be very useful."

"How do you know about this?'

"He told me."

"Well at least we know he doesn't keep secrets, and now we really can't go and accuse him, we'll just have to keep an eye on him."

"Will do."

Just then Imogen and Kitty had a strange but familiar feeling in their guts. it meant that Katt needed their help. They went out to the living room to meet everyone else, Katt was standing in the middle of the group ready to tell everyone about her problem.

"So what's the issue?" Imogen asked.

"Some girl flirted with Ricky." Katt yelled.

"Um, Okay well…" Imogen started.

"Drag her ass!" Rikki interrupted.

"You guys figure it out, I gotta get back to class." Just then Katt disappeared, they gathered together and looked at each other.

"She needs to drag that girl." RIkki repeated herself.

"I agree! Rick is off limits." Courtney said.

"But confrontation is so exhausting. Do we have to do that? That girl is probably really sorry she did it anyways." Zane said.

"She'll be sorry when we get done with her." Rikki said cracking her knuckles.

"Guys violence is not the answer." Imogen said.

"He's right, it's not really a good idea to let Katt's anger run amuck." Zac said.

"Why don't we just ask the girl to stop?" Imogen asked.

"That could come back later to bite us, and katt would come off as the jealous

type and could be confronted about it." Zane said.

"What if we tell her to stop and she doesn't?" Courtney asked.

"Good point Courtney, see talking won't work. We have to attack… her." Rikki

said.

"Can't we just ignore it?" Kitty asked.

"Apparently not when Ricky is Involved." Imogen said.

"Well then let's just do your idea get walked all over by some man stealer." Rikki said.

"Ricky's a nice guy so I doubt he would let anyone steal him. This is more about the girl then it is Ricky, so let's throw the possibility of him actually being stolen out the window." Imogen said.

"You know, being belligerent might just make things worse." Zane said.

"How?" Rikki asked.

"Ricky could see how much of a hot head Katt is and leave." Zane answered.

"No one saw that won't be coming." Zac said.

"Okay, how about we go along with Rikki's idea-" Imogen started.

"Yes!" Rikki interrupted.

"Let me finish, we will go along with Rikki's idea to confront her, there will be no violence." Imogen said.

"Half of a victory still counts as a victory, so I feel good." Rikki said.

"I hope it works out." Courtney said.

"I hate confrontation but majority rules and I don't much feel like going against it." Zane closed his book and went back to his room.

"He's just mad because I won." Rikki said.

"I don't think Zane gets mad, I feel like her just gets uncomfortable." Zac said.

"Oh what do *you* know new guy?" Rikki said.

"Enough to know that this conversation is over." Zac said, getting up and putting his headphones on and heading to his room.

"Leave it to Rikki to clear a room." Courtney laughed.

"Yup, I can tell that you and Zac will get along just fine." Imogen said.

"Yeah, whatever, just make sure you tell Katt that I won." Rikki said walking to her room.

"For what it's worth, it seems that Rikki has proven her usefulness." Courtney got up and returned to her room.

"She's not wrong." Kitty said.

"Yeah, yeah." Imogen said.

The both of them went back to their rooms. when Katt did come back, Imogen told her how their discussion went and Katt agreed and went with it. Zane sat in his room, Rikki was right Zane was upset but not that she had won, it was more of what they had decided on, he was worried about the backlash of katt confronting someone. Whether the situation went go or bad Katt was going to worry about it until it actually happened. Confrontation was physically and mentally uncomfortable for Katt, but at the same it times it was deemed necessary from time to time. Though the decision did bother him he decided not to say anything about it due to the fact that he didn't want to cause any more confrontation. He closed his book pulled the covers over his face and went to sleep.

Chapter 9: Because I'm my own enemy

"Katt, before you go can I talk to you about something?" Imogen asked.

"Sure, what's up?"

"Courtney is a little uncomfortable with Zac."

"That's fine, I understand her reasoning."

"What's the point of bringing things to your attention if you already know?"

"Who knows? maybe it's a courtesy to myself?"

"You're a weird person."

"What else is new?"

The next day Imogen came out to the living room to see only Rikki and Zac sitting there. This was something a little odd to see since Zane was almost always in the living room unless it was loud, but at the same time he thought that maybe Rikki was annoying him so he went back to his room.

"Where's Zane?" Imogen asked.

"Probably sulking from his defeat." Rikki smiled.

It's not that Rikki had never had her idea used before it just that it's never been taken over Zane's. Every time Zane had an idea that avoided confrontation it always won over hers, or at least that's what she thought, the real reason was that Rikki's idea's always involved katt doing things that would get her in serious trouble, arrested or dead. But to her for once Zane's cowardly ways had failed proving that her was was right and that no matter who was added into the group she could still be useful.

"I haven't seen him since the discussion." Zac said.

"That's a little weird, hope he's okay." Imogen thought it'd be best to not bother him, he wasn't sure what this could possibly be doing to Zane, he knew he would probably take on stress but wasn't aware of how the much stress there was so he decided he would possibly check on him later.

"Well, he's like a turtle, he gets scared and goes back into his shell." Rikki said.

"Lay off him Rikki." Imogen said, she was starting to get annoyed with her gloating.

"Yeah, Zane's not a coward he just doesn't want any more trouble than he needs." Zac said.

"If you say so. Confrontation is inevitable and he should just accept it." Rikki said.

"He's aware of just doesn't go looking for trouble, unlike you, lay off him, this is your last warning." Imogen said.

"Whatever." Rikki got up and walked to her room.

"So where is Zane?" Zac asked.

"You assume I know?" Imogen asked.

"I know you know, after we answered you got quiet for a second."

"Well you're right, he probably sleeping off Katt's excessive stress."

"What a burden."

"We all have them."

Just then Katt appeared in the living room.

"How did it go?" Zac asked.

"Eh, it went. She seemed to understand so whether I had said something or not it would have been fine." Katt said.

"Do you think you overrated?" Imogen asked.

"Probably." Katt said.

"Are you feeling okay otherwise?" Zac asked.

"Yeah, for the most part." Katt said.

"Good." Zac said.

Katt sat down in a chair with everyone else and didn't talk, that all sad in silence. Imogen had never seen katt like this, she was normally so full of life, but now she seemed a little dead inside, but he chalked it up to her have a bad day. Over the next couple of days, it seemed like everyone was groggy, except Zac. Imogen was tired and drained, he couldn't really friend a point to do anything. Rikki barely touched her guitar, and almost never left her room. Zane didn't feel like reading at all, Country was sad all the time. Even Kitty was feeling the effects and it started to worry her. Katt had stopped show up all together it was as if everyone was becoming, Except Zac. Kitty called Katt into her room.

"You rang?" Katt said.

"Yeah, what's going on out there?" Kitty asked.

"Nothing?"

"Don't you think that's an issue?"

"No."

"Think about it, you haven't felt anything need for us in weeks?"

"is that a bad thing."

"Of course, if you keep going on like this e will cease to exist."

"I mean, I guess."

Katt was like a zombie now, living life as if she couldn't see the point. she seemed to just walk through it without noticing others. Before Kitty could finish the conversation katt has disappeared. She didn't care to hear the rest of what Kitty had to say. Kitty was nervous about this, so she went to talk to Imogen about it.

"Have you noticed anything strange around here?" Kitty asked.

"Strange? Yes, actually, everything a bit slow."

"Good, you're aware, because I don't think the other three are aware."

"Yeah, I've been feeling pretty tired lately."

"I could tell."

"Do you know what's causing it?"

"I think I might have a good idea."

"Have you walked to Katt?"

"She won't listen."

"Well, that could spell something bad for us."

"Yeah, We'll just have to deal with it for right now until I can figure out exactly what's going on and how to fix it."

"Got it."

Chapter 10: Because my Brain is a scary place

Zac Started to notice that no one was ever out the living room anymore. He unlike the others he was happy about it. "Good." He thought, no more of those pesky emotions to mess with Katt. This wasn't something he was expecting but he was still glad about it. Zane's books were no blank, Rikki's guitar no longer made noise, Courtney's lava lamps stopped working. Little by little the house was falling apart but no one was bother by it other than Imogen and Kitty. Zac was siphoning off their energy and getting stronger. When Katt ever did show up she went straight to Zac anyone one else. Zac's room had even started to change, his door was now a double door with a medical sign over it. The room itself had seem to have doubled in size. He had a California king sized bed and more speakers than before, it was almost too big. Katt entered his room and he gestured her to have a seat in his room. He had also gain control of his music and was able to pretty much control how Katt felt, but from time to time the outside word for overpower him.

"What seems to be the problem."

"I don't remember."

"Good."

"But I want to remember."

"Why? the outside world is meaningless, don't worry about it emotions are useless anyways."

"No, everyone has them."

"But you're not everyone else now are you Katt?"

"No."

"Correct. everyone else is normal, They can be happy on their own, you can't."

"I can't?"

"Right, you lost that privilege because you were born defective."

"Defective...?"

"Right, you're sisters came out fine but not you."

"I'm the screw up."

"Yes, and why do you think that is?"

"Because I was born defective?"

"Exactly, that's why you will never be like others, because you are broken."

"I'm broken?"

"Maybe you should off yourself."

"I don't want to to."

"Why are you wasting your time, Living and being a burden to everyone around you. Your family hates you and they ignore you, you better off dead."

"But it would hurt my mom."

"You think your mom loves you?"

"Of course."

"You not even the first born, you can tell by her mistreatment of you, she loves your sister more."

"No, they love me."

"When? When you sit there like a robot and kiss their asses? That's not love, they didn't even be you were sick."

"It doesn't matter; they love me I know it."

"I bet they'd believe you were sick if you killed yourself."

"You're right."

"I know I'm right, I'm your medicine, I'm always right."

"I should just kill myself."

"Exactly, good idea."

"How?"

"You're the creative one, figure it out."

Katt got up and left his room, she had a good idea of what she was going to do now and have completely gotten why she had decided to seek help anyway. this was always how her meetings with him went. she didn't talk to the others because she felt distant from them. she was starting to feel as though the others were too emotional. therefore, they were too annoying for her to be around right now, because they were parts of her and Zac was medicine so he he couldn't be gone, he was supposed to be good for her. Katt had become dull, no longer full of life and so easily swayed, it was as if truly her will to live was gone and she wasn't quite sure why she was still alive. The more powerful Zac became the more he'd been corrupted, he had lost sight of why he was actually there in the first place. Instead of helping her, he was just making her feel like crap. This was also due the fact that Katt's sister caused her so much stress that Katt would also have to up her dosage form time to time just to cope with the tension. This added more stress. Kitty and Imogen watched the zombie like Katt walk out of Zac's room. she was hunched over and then eventually she collapsed under the weight of her own despair. They quickly picked her up and ran her back to Imogen's room before they could be seen by anyone else. They laid her down in his bed, she was barely conscious.

"Katt can you hear me?" Imogen said

Katt's eyes had opened a little but it didn't seem like she was aware of anyone's presence or even her own.

"She's worse than I thought." Kitty said.

"So then what do we do now?" Imogen asked.

"Let her sleep for now, it looks like she hasn't slept in a while so maybe when she wakes up she'll be in her right mind." Kitty said.

"I'm doubting it. it looks like she's been brainwashed or something." Imogen said.

"Yeah, we have to snap her out if it before things get worse."

"Can things get worse?" Suddenly there was a knock at the door, Imogen opened it to fine RIkki standing there.

"Yes?" Imogen asked.

"I can't get into my room."

"What do you mean?"

"While I was laying in my bed I was yanked out of my room and the door shot itself and locked before I could get back in." Rikki had looked sick, she didn't yell or anything like that even the fire in her eyes had once been filled with had been smothered and drowned in the darkness that was becoming Katt's mind.

"Okay go sit in Zane's room, I'm sure he won't mind." Imogen said curious to hear her answer.

"Okay, that's fine." Rikki walked away with nothing else to say.

"Why'd you send her away?" Kitty asked.

"We have enough issues and the less people now the easier this is the keep this quiet. they they come back I'll send them to Courtney's room. we just need to keep them all together right now."

"True, worst case we'll have to send them to my room, they can't get locked out of theirs cause I'm the only one whose isn't made up."

"Okay, so in the meantime what do we do?"

"Um...let her sleep and try not to disappear in the process."

"That seems almost impossible."

"You have me even if you do disappear, I am moving and too much for Katt, Even Zac cannot change me."

"So I can believe that it will be okay no matter what? that's a relief."

"That's what I'm here for."

Imogen opened his door again to make sure no one was out there. The coast was clear and that put him even more at ease. Imogen knew he was swayed by Zac's powers and it made him feel a bit unnerved. But he knew that Kitty would work hard to make sure he wouldn't be caught again. There was a knock at his door again, this time it was Courtney, with the same issue Rikki had, he sent her to Zane's room like he did Rikki.

"We gotta move fast." He said to Kitty.

"Well we're on someone else's schedule so I don't know what you want from me." Kitty said pointed at the sleeping Katt. Katt's body began to disappear.

"She's leaving! why is she leaving?" Imogen started to panic.

"Someone could be waking her up in the real world or maybe she's entering deep sleep, I don't know, if I did I would be way more important than this."

"What do we do?"

"Let her go, she's not useful to us this way anyways so it doesn't matter. we need her awake and alert."

"How the hell are we supposed to catch her again."

"Hell, if I know."

"You don't have to an idea what you're doing do you?"

"Sorry this has never happened before; she has never put anything in her body
that changes her brain chemistry, the most she did was talk allergy medicine. And I don't see you coming up with anything."

"Valid point."

"We'll grab her again I'm sure."

Imogen went out to check on the others, Courtney's door was slowly losing its color and Rikki's door was slowly starting to break. As he was heading towards Zane's room the door opened and threw Rikki, Zane, and Courtney right at him. like Rikki and Courtney both said described the room threw them out and the door shut itself and locked.

"Now where do we stay?" Zane whined.

"Go to Kitty's room." Imogen said.

"What if it does the same thing?" Rikki asked.

"It won't." Imogen reassured her.

The group got up and walked across the living room to Kitty's room. Imogen has noticed that even the Living hand even been affected by Katt's sadness. What was once a joyous room where everyone had fun and even quarreled had become so sad and depressing, everyone's chairs were turning white then to gray until they were completely black and rotted. It was a creepy and uncomfortable sight for him, everyone's except Zac's chair was affected. Imogen thought about how he had promised Courtney that he was going to protect her, now look at everything. He felt bad for not keeping his promise, he should have saw what was happening before it was too late, thought he knew this wasn't the time to think about it he still felt bad. He put the thought in the back of his mind when he returned to the room.

"If I leave you know you'll be thrown out of your room too." Kitty said sensing that Imogen wanted to be alone.

"I know, it's okay I wasn't going to ask you to leave anyways, we need someplace to come up with a plan." Imogen said.

"Well maybe they will wake up. I'm not sure how much longer they will last through."

"What happening to them?"

"It seems like she's disconnecting or something like that, something or someone is making her feel that we are irrelevant and no longer needed."

"Wasn't this inevitable?"

"Not exactly if it was her, then it wouldn't be this sad and scary, we would have a glorious and sweet send off, this is just fucked man."

"Yeah, I guess you're right, this really sucks. how do we stop it?"

"For now stay in our rooms for all Zac knows since their doors are gone he only has us to deal with. but I'm sure he's not aware that I am unmoving, so let's keep it that way, so we'll just hang out in here, until I go see him."

"Do you wanna go?"

"I could, it would be scary but I could."

"Maybe it would be better that way then, you know man to man."

"But he would never hurt a little girl."

"Your right, go for it."

"If you were scary why did you offer yourself."

"It's the nice thing to do."

"Not, if you don't mean it asshole."

"Well why don't we decide it another way…" Kitty quickly put her finger on her nose. "Nose goes"

"Dammit!" Imogen exclaimed, now we had to go and he was very scared, he opened his door and walked straight to Zac's room, thinking back he would have had to go anyways, because if kitty would have left he would have been kicked out of his room. it wouldn't have mattered if he had volunteered he was already screwed. he knocked on the door, it opened and Zac pointed to a chair for him to sit in.

"Hello Zac, how are things going?"

"Hello Imogen, things are going well."

"Really?"

"Yeah, I've been been able to help katt a lot."

"Really? you've seen Katt?"

"Yeah, she comes here often."

"That's interesting, I've barely seen her."

"Well maybe she doesn't need you guys anymore."

"Why would you think that?"

"You guys are just figments of imagination, you're not actually different people your just carbon copies of her."

"That may be true, but you should be true to yourself."

"What is she 5? how can she stay like this when she's not even normal, she's nothing but a broken person."

"She's not broken! she's never been that way."

"Yeah, she is that's why I'm here to make her like normal people."

"She was normal."

"No, having people in your brain isn't normal, it's barely sane."

"It was normal to her, and that' what's matters. Katt isn't a great person, she's just different, so what if she doesn't have it all together, who does? She's fine."

"Not by society's standards. To the outside world she's a very sick girl, she's needs me."

"You call this normal? look around you she closing us out, she's going numb, normal person have feelings."

"Normal people have can control their feelings and don't have to use such tactics."

"Well it's not like she ever wanted to be normal in the first place, that's what makes her so great, you didn't have her from herself, as a matter that you're making her worse."

"Well it doesn't matter what you think so you'll be gone too."

"Oh is that so?"

"Yup, just like the others, you pesky feelings will soon be gone forever."

During that moment Imogen had realized something that even Kitty had never thought of. he wasn't a feeling like the other three, he was her alter-ego, and her conscious, he couldn't disappear even if he wanted too because like kitty he had a direct unchanging connection to her, If Kitty was the Id and katt was the ego then Imogen was the superego. and every human had those.

"Yeah, us pesky feelings sure but how are you going to go about killing us?"

"That's the best part about this! I don't have to get my hands dirty, Katt will do it for me, it didn't even take much."

"Whelp, since you're so smart I guess you have everything figured out."

"You won't get rid of me like you did Tak."

"How do you know about Tak?"

"I've been looking through Katt's brain for a while now, did you think Tak was gone for good? ha, everyone has darkness in their hearts. Tak may not be able to form a body but that doesn't mean that she isn't around."

"Well that just made this conversation more interesting."

"Wow Katt didn't tell you?"

"If she didn't know she was making you, how would she know about that, let's be honest she is Katt."

"You have a good point."

"Well I'm gonna go now, um your plain will be foiled... and all that good stuff. soo buy now."

"Right... yeah, you will lose and all will be lost blah blah blah..."

Imogen didn't know when the moment had become so awkward but he knew he had to get out of the current situation. He thought the ending for that conversation would be more heroic or something like that and felt really embarrassed that it wasn't, he walked back to his room feeling a bit confused.

Chapter 11: Because I will survive

"Good to see you back in once piece." Kitty said.

"Yeah, it got weird so I left."

"Got weird? What do you mean weird?"

"Like the conversation got kind of friendly…"

"How did that happen?"

"I'm not quite sure actually."

"Never mind, did you find out anything."

"Um, he's trying to get Katt to get rid of all of us, um Tak is still alive, He knows about Tak, and I won't foil his plans etc..." Imogen said trailing off.

"Um… Tak is still alive…? Well I could believe that."

"Am I the only one surprised by this?"

"Well that kind of darkness doesn't just go away, Katt must be finding another way to to let can't so she can't take form."

"Is that actually possible?"

"Yeah, so instead of hurting real people Katt could be, I don't know killing sims off or something."

"Sounds like Katt."

"Yup, but um…Oh no he's trying to destroy us, and get Katt to commit suicide. We need to go warn the others."

"Yeah we do, lets juts hope their up to it, I'm a bit worried that they might not be up for it they been a little off lately."

Imogen closed the door and went to Kitty's room. Something had to be done about the Zac. Imogen opened the door to find they were all sleeping. Zane was curled up in Kitty's bed, Rikki was stretched out on the floor and Courtney look extremely comfortable in a bean bag chair, Imogen went over and woke Zane up.

"What is it?" Zane said rubbing his eyes.

"Grab Courtney, I'll pick up Rikki." Imogen Instructed.

"Why?"

"Do you want to be the one to wake Rikki up?"

"I'm gonna go grab Courtney."

The boys picked the girls up and headed to Imogen's room. Rikki was never nice when she woke up and Courtney was just a hard sleeper. Imogen felt that it would be time better spent to wake her while they were all together and in a safer environment. He also thought that Kitty would do a better job at waking Rikki up because she was afraid of her like the others were. They dropped the girls in Imogen's bed. Imogen and and stood by Courtney and kitty walked to the other side to be by Rikki.

"What a pain." Zane said.

"You could have Rikki." Kitty said.

"True. So how do we wake Courtney up?" Zane asked.

"With a kiss from her true love." Kitty giggled.

"Shut up." Zane said looking down at Courtney, normally they shook her but he felt too tired for that, it took too much energy that he didn't have. He held her to and she instinctively opened her mouth. Imogen cover her moth and she pooped up gasping for air. She looked around furiously and then pointed her anger towards the boys, they then pointed at a sleeping Rikki next to her. Courtney seeing the danger got out the bed at quickly as possible and hid behind Imogen. Imogen then nodded at kitty and pointed at a booking laying on his dresser, Kitty walked over to it and angled her arms perfectly and threw the book at Rikki's face. Rikki woke up furiously looking around the the Tasmanian devil, really to take someone. They backed away more until she figured out that she was no longer in the place that she had fallen asleep.

"What the hell guys?"

"Someone had to wake you up and Kitty lost as nose goes." Zane said.

"So you threw a book at me?" Rikki said still angry.

"Well your awake now aren't you?" Kitty asked.

"You should be nicer to be I'm a delicate person." Rikki laughed.

"In what world?" Imogen asked. Rikki's eyes darted to him full of fire, she quickly pulled a match out of her pocket, showing that she was prepared to burn his room down to the ground, Imogen put his hands up in surrender.

"Woah, be easy, I was joking just like you were." He said hesitantly.

"I'm just busting your balls man." Her face lightened up and she started to laugh.

"Glad to see we're all in a mostly good mood but jokes aside things are getting pretty bad out there." Kitty said. Imogen nodded.

"Yeah, we've never lost our rooms before, this is getting pretty scary." Courtney said.

"Zac's got a bit of God status and Katt is on his side, well brainwashed is the better word for it." Kitty said.

"I knew it! Called it." Courtney said.

"You knew?" Rikki said, sounding disgusted.

"It's more of I had a bad feeling this would happen." Courtney replied.

"Did you know about this?" Zane asked Imogen. Rikki and Zane started at Imogen waiting for an answer. Imogen looked down avoiding their sight, he knew he had let Courtney down.

"So you did know. And didn't tell anyone?" Rikki yelled at him.

"It's that I just ignored it, katt brushed it off, and Kitty said that we couldn't run in guns blazing accusing him of things he had not yet done." Imogen felt ashamed of himself.

"Lay off him." Kitty said stepping in front of Imogen.

"So you both screwed us?" Zane said.

"Of course we were the last ones to know right?" Rikki said.

"If we could have seen thigs coming we would have stopped it. But I can't predict the future." Kitty said.

Rikki looked at Imogen and Kitty and sighed. She had never felt so left out before She knew that something was up but she never thought it was something like this. how could they keep such a dangerous secret from her? Was it a trust issues, has she done something to make then think that she was disloyal? Zane felt betrayed, not by the others but by Zac. He had hoped that Zac wouldn't have turned out to be evil and that they could spend more time together, they were great friends and he made Zane feel like he wasn't alone. It wasn't that Zane didn't like the others they just didn't understand him the way Zac did. He could see that the others were different and different wasn't bad it it wasn't the same. Zane felt a bit heart broken. Courtney had no feelings, she had knowing this so why feel surprised or anything else. Five people was Katt's limit, if Courtney could figure it out then why couldn't Katt?

"Why is it that anyone who isn't us causes these types of issues for Katt?" Courtney asked.

"I'm guessing because she's stretching herself too thing, she not meant for this and I'm sure it exerts a lot of mental energy for us to be here too. so five people are her limits. That's why the others are unknown to her, she avoided Tak and Zac was being made without her even being aware of it." Kitty said.

"Makes sense." Imogen said.

"So what do we do?" Zane asked.

"We're going to stand up to Zac before it's too late." Imogen answered.

"Too late?" Courtney asked.

"Yeah, he's got Katt contemplating suicide and I fear that one more push could make her stop thinking and start taking action." Kitty said sounded worried.

"Holy Crap and if Katt dies we die." Rikki yelled."

"Bingo." Imogen said.

They all knew what they had to do, Sort of, they knew they had to stop Zac, but weren't sure how. It's not like they were the power rangers or Voltron or something like that. They couldn't just combine their rings and make captain planet through that would be a sight that everyone would want to see. They walked to Zac's door with barely any confidence in their step. They knew that their end could come at any time so they need to get this done quickly so they could rescue katt. They door opened on its own and they wall walked in.

"Look who's still alive." Zac chuckled.

"It's gonna take a lot more then this to do away with us." Zane said.

"Also we die, you die… doesn't that bother you?" Rikki asked.

"No, Prozac is an anti-depressant that is disturbed everywhere. So who cares if I die? Unlike you guys I'm not unique, there are literally multiples of me." Zac said.

"What is this? some even plan orchestrated by doctors to cause the genocide of depressed people?" Courtney was hysterical.

"Woah, whoa, no one said anything about genocide." Zac sounded nervous.

"But you said-"Zane started.

"No, No I know what I said., and it wasn't all that, I can promise you that much. I don't know what I'm like in other people's bodies. Maybe I went rouge, I don't know but no genocide." Zac sounded uncomfortable. He was just trying to kill them and Katt, but not all depressed people, that was over kill. He was just supposed to make katt feel better but slipped over to the dark side and figured it wasn't all bad.

"Okay, so totally destruction of people with mental illness is not the goal?" Imogen asked.

"No, not at all. I'm not heartless, maybe a monster but not heartless." Zac stood by his already screwed up principles.

"Oh, well, that took everything away from how I was going to confront you…I got nothing." Courtney put her hands up in surrender like fashion.

"Well that was interesting." Zac laughed.

"Regardless of that we're gonna stop you from hurting Katt." Rikki said.

"How?" Zac laughed.

Just then katt walked into the room, she was coming to see Zac for one final time, and was amazed to see everyone there.

"What are you all doing here?" Katt asked.

"We're here to stop you from making a huge mistake Katt!" Imogen said.

"Yeah! Please don't harm yourself any longer, you deserve to be here just as much as anyone else." Courtney said.

"Also killing yourself is a lot of effort, and do you really want to do all of that?" Zane asked.

"Zane!" Kitty yelled at him.

"I'm not wrong. Not to mention katt what about you mom? You love your mom am I right?" Zane asked.

"Yeah I do… I guess."

"And what about Ricky?" Courtney asked.

"What's the point of getting into a relationship and wanted to be have a future with him if your gonna end it this way?" Imogen asked.

"Stop that." Zac demanded.

"Offing yourself is selfish, why do you get to leave and cause everyone around you pain?" Rikki asked.

"Stop that! You're trash, Katt you're defective trash and no one will ever love you the way you want to be loved!" Zac yelled.

"Well…" Katt started looking down at the floor.

"Katt if someone isn't loving you right then tell them how to love you and care for you." Imogen said.

"And if they don't want to then fuck em." Rikki said.

"Your mom always says closed mouth doesn't get feed right?" Courtney laughed.

"NO! no one understands you Katt! So why stick around?" Zac said, he was livid.

"He's right, no one gets me, it's so hard." Katt said.

"Not everyone knows how to deal with people with mental illness Katt." Kitty said.

"They could be scared, they don't know how to deal with you, but they could learn. And eventually they will, they will need time." Imogen said.

"Also do you want to die before graduating high school?" Zane asked.

"You're not good at being helpful are you Zane?" Katt laughed.

"Neither are you, that's why I'm like this, not feel better so I can read books again."

Everyone started to gather around Katt and gave her a group hug. Katt felt walk inside. she couldn't believe that she had even though of such a terrible thing. The room around them started to shrink, Zac's speakers started to break down and crumble, his "Throne" became a small old wooden chair. Zac watched as the room got smaller and smaller, the trouble door was now a single one. The others watched and started stepping out of the room one by one eventually leaving only Katt and Zac.

"Thanks for the the help Zac, but I don't think I need you anymore." Katt said.

"But I'm psychological drug! You can't just quit me." Zac yelled.

"Watch me." Katt walked out of the now closet sized room, the door shut behind her and locked.

"I'm really sorry guys." Katt said.

"Eh. Don't stress it." Imogen said.

"Why didn't he explode?" Rikki asked.

"Probably because he's technically still in my system." Katt said.

"So are you gonna stop taking Prozac" Zane asked.

"Yeah, needing medicine to be happy makes me feel uncomfortable. it's just not right for me." Katt said.

"So how do we fix this?" Zane said, jiggling the handle of his locked door.

"Sorry. And I'm just going to stop taking my medicine." Katt pointed at the doorknob and it unlocked.

"That's probably dangerous." Kitty said.

"Probably." Katt said. She knew that this could be bad for her but she need this out of her body as soon as possible so she could get back to her normal self. So what she was a dork? There was nothing wrong with that. she would meet people who would get to use it. Katt felt a little worried about how Ricky would feel but if he truly loved then he would prefer it this way. They were right, people can change and lean to love Katt for who she was, whether she was happy or sad.

"It's not your fault you're like this." Kitty said.

"If it's was, you wouldn't be like this." Imogen said.

"Yeah, it's too much work, both you and I know that, I mean who actually wants to feel back all the time." Zane said.

"Holy crap when did you get there?" Katt stiffened.

"I only wanted my room unlocked so I could go get a book, but the better question is how do you scare yourself in your own brain?" Zane asked.

"I don't know." Katt said.

"Are you really questioning this? I mean Katt's brain is probably the strangest place in the world. It's like the freaking twilight zone in here." Rikki said.

"Doubting that, this is more of a giant game of the sims, only you guys don't eat or use the bathroom, which is a great think because I don't want crap in my head." Katt said.

"We don't need to use the bathroom, because Zac was the crap," Rikki said, "So now your gonna stop being stupid now right?"

"Yeah, I'm doing doing awful things, getting off my meds will be rough though." Katt said.

"Yeah, good luck with that." said Rikki.

"I just want the record to show that I knew it." Courtney said trying to lighten the mood.

"Yeah, I'm sorry for not listening." Katt said. They all hugged. Katt left feeling happy, she felt like he life could start moving again after being at a standstill and that she could finally be herself. Though she had no idea what was to come from immediate stop of taking physiological drugs but she would see find out.

Chapter 12: Because bouncing back is hard

What Katt didn't realize is that her body had become dependent on Prozac, make it a little harder for he to quit it.

"I don't really feel well" Katt said walking into Imogen's room.

"What type of feeling well?" Imogen asked

"My head hurts a lot."

"Well did you think this would be a cake walk?"

"Well no, but I'm sad in pain"

"Well why don't you lay down?"

"Everything makes me want to cry."

"Yeah, that sounds about right."

"I don't want to deal with people anymore."

"You know you can't do that, right?"

"Yes I can." Katt wrapped herself in a blanket.

"if you're trying to avoid people Zane would be the person to bother. I'm not here for your pouting Katt." Imogen sounded annoyed, He knew Katt would get like this but he still hated it. Katt hated change and this was a big one, she had a long way before she would get the drug fully out of her system. She knew that herself. Katt wasn't the brat that people made her out to be, she actually had a decent amount of discipline. It was the fact that decent amount was attached to Katt's unsolicited funky attitude. Imogen turned around to see Katt gone. He was relieved that she had left, he couldn't deal with her like Zane could.

"Hi Zane." Katt plopped into his his bed right next to him.

"Hello." He said not looking up from his book.

"Do I ever scare you?"

"Do you ever use a door is a better question."

"Shut up."

"Why are you here? What's up?"

"My head hurts, I'm sad and I no longer want to deal with people. Imogen made me go away."

"So you came here?"

"Yea, you wouldn't give me crappy actual advice that I need to hear."

"That's because you didn't make me that way, you made me to help you deal with the fact that you actually hate people, but know that they have to exists for you to exists."

"Great exposition. Wanna tell the readers anything else?"

"Nope, I think they get me enough. I bet I'm their favorite."

"So how do I fix this?"

"Why do you ask for advice you don't really want."

"I'm not quite sure."

"If you don't want to deal with people then just don't. it is really that hard." Zane sighed.

"Of course it is."

"How? You do a fairly good job of not going outside."

"Are you made for anxiety or to give me the business?"

"No, no, that's Imogen and Kitty's huge job."

"You're not wrong."

"So what's really wrong?"

"I just don't feel kay, and I don't know why."

"Sometimes it's just like that."

"No, everything has a reason."

"You're right, the reason is that you have a chemical imbalance in your brain, is that good enough?"

"No."

"if you don't want random down moments then I can't help you."

"Someone has too."

"You have depression, deal with it. I know it's hard to swallow, but eat it."

"I did eat it."

"Are you sure?"

"What do you mean?"

"You seem to think that the meds would "cure" you, they are more of the and aid. Granted they aren't the type of aid you needed, but it's not a full recovery you have to do some of it yourself. Maybe you should talk to someone."

"I don't want no one in my business."

"Just talk to Ricky, he makes everything feel better, right?"

"That's because he's adorable."

"Gross, go bother Courtney with that, you two could probably go one forever about that crap."

"Sorry." Katt wrapped herself I her covers, "Being like this is hard."

"Yeah, yeah, we know, but this is you." Zane closed his book and went to return it to the bookshelf and grab another.

"What are you gonna read now?" She asked.

"Fantasy."

Katt laid down in his bed and got comfy, she wasn't planning on sleeping but she ended up there for what seemed like centuries. She couldn't understand why she was so tired, she hadn't felt this way in a while. Her body wasn't cold but she couldn't stop shaking. She found it hard to stay still. No matter how many covers she wrapped herself in she just couldn't warm up.

Chapter 13: Because I'm Recovering

"You guys notice anything wired." Imogen asked.

"Weird like its snowing but warm in here?" Zane asked nonchalantly.

"Well, yeah, pretty much." Imogen said.

"How could we not notice this?" Rikki said sounded annoying.

"Just want make sure it wasn't just me" Imogen said.

Kitty looked around and Immediately for for katt. She appeared instantly looking very weak and sick.

"What happening?" Courtney asked.

"I'm freezing but I can't stop sweating." Katt said.

"Are you okay?" Imogen asked.

"What do you think?" Katt snapped back.

"No need to bite my head off," Imogen said.

"Is this something kind of sickness?" Zane asked.

"I don't know, this has never happened before and yesterday I tossed my cookies." Katt said.

"Tossed your cookies?" the room filled with Rikki's laughter.

"Yeah, it feels weird to say puke or throw up or more of gross… my mom and dad used to say "tossed cookies" so I say it." Katt said.

"You're a child, you know that right?" Rikki laughed and pointed lie a cliché bully. Katt was not amused.

"Maybe you should go to the hospital, you almost never throw up." Kitty said.

"No, no… then they will poke me with needles. And you know how much I hate IV's." Katt started to pout.

"Well you can't stay like this." Imogen said

"Yeah, Yeah, I know." Katt walked towards Rikki's room.

"Um excuse me? Where do you think you're going?" Rikki asked.

"You're excused, and to go and get in your bed, it's the host in the house due to the fact that you're such a hot head." Katt closed the door behind her.

"I hate this." Rikki said pulling out her matches.

"Get used to it, she does it to everyone, what makes you so special?" Zane asked.

"Can it." Rikki said.

"She probably wouldn't have done it if you hadn't have made fun of her." Imogen said.

"Ugh." Rikki dropped another lit match on the floor.

"How are we going to make Katt feel better." Country asked.

"We can't, she has to get through this on her own." Zane said.

"When did you become the expert?" Rikki snapped.

"You're just annoyed with everyone today aren't you, little miss sunshine?" Zane snapped back.

"I think he's right, somethings we can't fix, this is more of a body thing, Not mental. Not matter how we make Katt feel, her body will be sick." Kitty said.

They all felt kind of bad that Katt felt so sick, but at the same time Kitty was right. Unfortunately, Katt had quit psychological medicine and there was no way she was going to get off scot free. What Katt was experiencing was withdrawal, she had the sakes and couldn't keep anything down. It worried her mother to the point that she was almost afraid to leave the house. Recovery was going to be a tough road for Katt but she would get through it eventually.

Chapter 14: Because I'm Me

After a couple more weeks of sickness Katt was finally back to normal, though she had wasted her whole winter break in bed she was happy that she was back to normal. Soon she would be applying for college and she was pretty sure that bad attendance might be something that would matter to the people in the admissions department.

"I don't want to do all this." Katt wined.

"Do you ever come here just to say "hello"?" Rikki asked. "or is that not a thing?"

"Are you ever in a good mood? Or is that not a thing?" Katt said.

"Shut up." Rikki said.

"Why do I keep you around?" Katt asked.

"I ask myself the same question every waking moment of my life." Rikki said.

"So what's the issue."

"I don't want to apply to college, I don't really want to graduate." Katt said.

"But you hate high school." Zane said.

"Maybe I should rephrase this. I'm not ready to leave high school, yes I hate it but leaving will be so uncomfortable. everything will change, I will have to make new friends, and meet new people and talk to strangers."

"Oh no, the real world is so scary." Rikki mocked.

"Shut it." Imogen said.

"I agree with Katt, that all sounds like a lot of work, can't we just stay home." Zane said.

"No, you know we can't stay home, mom is nuts. And Katt, it will be fine, you will make new friends, hone you skills and learn how to speak Japanese." Kitty said.

"But I suck at languages." Katt said. She was not wrong, she had failed French, and Latin, and for some strange reason always in her second year.

"But you hated those languages, and you love Japan. Also high school has to end, if you're there longer then you should be people will think you're not smart. And your sister graduated in four years." Imogen hated throwing the sister card out but it always worked.

"I would just rather not do this. College seems fun but I would have to get out to the house." Katt said.

"Well you don't like to be bothered anyways." Zane said.

"What about Ricky!" Katt yelled.

"That's what this is really about." Imogen said.

"Well you and Ricky will be fine. Distance makes the heart grow fonder. And you'll see him during break." Courtney said.

"But I'll miss him and we'll both be so busy. What if something bad happens?" Katt started to cry.

"Nothing bad will happen unless you think it will, he's a nice guy and you know that." Courtney said.

"What if he finds someone else."

"He won't."

"But."

"If he does then screw him?" Rikki said.

"It seems like a lot of work for him to dump you after high school." Zane said.

"Not if he finds out how crazy she is, if I were him, I would head for the hills." Rikki said.

"Not helping." Imogen said.

"Well, he's got a good idea of you guys." Katt said.

"You told him about us? No wonder you're worried! You better start giving those hoodies back, cause he's probably looking for someone better now."

"Rikki!" Imogen said.

"What?! We're here to stop her from making bad decisions and then she just hauls off and makes them anyways, what are we here for if she's just gonna be stupid?" Rikki said.

"Well…how did it go?" Zane asked.

"Well… he didn't freak out; he was just cool about it." Katt said.

"Because he's Ricky and he loves you." Cortney said.

"Yeah… that's true…"

"Have you talked to him about leaving for college? I mean you don't plan on going that far. "Courtney said.

"Well… he said he's not good at long distance relationships."

"That's it, game over!" Rikki said.

"But… he said we could make it work." Katt said.

"So everything's fine. You're fine, He's fine." Courtney said.

"But I won't get any kisses from him." Katt pouted.

"Then stay home, wait for him to finish high school, then go off to college together or don't. It all sounds like work." Zane said

"I feel like I need to work on how helpful you guys aren't, starting to forget why I need you around." Katt said.

"That means you're growing up." Zane snickered.

"You're trash, but you're my trash." Katt laughed.

"So do you feel better?" Courtney asked.

"Yup" Katt said.

Katt sat there with them and looked at them. She really loved her friends, even if she was talking to herself, she was a head case. As her senior year came and went katt was able to get into her top college. And has been enjoying her time ever sense, she ended up taking Japanese as a major along with writing and it is all going very well. She's on track to go to Japan and graduate on time. Her and Ricky were fine and stayed together, though they had some rocky moments, but what relationship doesn't. though she still has some down moments she keeps her depression and actually in check by doing things that make her happy. She made plenty of friends and they love her for who she is. As they should.

THE END